EDDIE

CARL

Story: NORMA SIMON

HOW DO I FEEL?

Pictures: JOE LASKER

Albert Whitman & Company ▪ Morton Grove, Illinois

To Carl Memling

E   Simon, Norma.
S   How do I feel? Pictures: Joe Lasker.   A. Whitman
         [c1970]

         1 v. (unpaged) illus.

         A book about the feelings of children—anger, frustration,
         weariness, pride, etc.

         1. Emotions—Fiction. 2. Picture books for children. I. Title.

X06664   E
LJ Cards, c1970   –P

Standard Book Number 8075-3414-5.
Library of Congress Card Number 77-126430.
Text © 1970 by Norma Simon; Illustrations © 1970 by Joe Lasker.
Published in 1970 by Albert Whitman & Company,
6340 Oakton Street, Morton Grove, Illinois 60053.
Published simultaneously in Canada by
General Publishing, Limited, Toronto.
Printed in the United States of America.
20   19   18   17   16   15   14   13

WHAT DO WE DO AND SAY?

WHEN you share with children what happens in this picture book to Carl and his twin brother, Eddie, try pausing after the question "How do I feel?" Listen to the answers you hear before reading the words in the book. You will find the children around you are telling you about their feelings. It is not accidental that this book invites participation. It was planned to do this.

A beginning book about feelings provides a natural introduction to the subjective sensations, reactions, and emotions that all people experience. If at an early age children understand that feelings are important and can be expressed in words, this may help in learning to live in our stressful world.

The most complex kind of communication between people involves the identification, verbalization, and articulation of feelings. At the base of many of our responses, intellectual and emotional, and our ability to relate to others is our capacity to label our own emotions. Giving a name to an emotion is frequently a first step to dealing with it.

In the subtle interaction of daily life, children watch and model themselves after the people around them. Eventually many of the reactions of others become a part of one's own behavior. To say this in another way, all the people who influence us in childhood become in a sense part of our adult selves. In a boy's life, the men he knows best will help determine the kind of man he will grow to be. For many boys, these men are not necessarily their fathers. For the twins in this picture book, it is Grandpa and Mike who provide models to follow. Yet even with the same models, each twin develops his own unique personality, as do children in most families.

If Carl and Eddie can suggest to children ways to name and be comfortable with their own feelings, then perhaps it will be possible for girls and boys to enjoy feeling "special, very special."

NORMA SIMON

We all live in Grandma and Grandpa's house.
Eddie, me, and my big brother Mike.
Eddie is my twin.
Me—I'm Carl.

I hear Grandpa's alarm clock.
How do I feel?
Lazy.

That Eddie!
Up and ready to go.
I tell him, "Eddie, you're so different.
Not like me."
That's what I tell that Eddie.

I smell Grandma's cooking.
How do I feel?
Hungry.

Eddie is first again.
I tell him, "Oh, Eddie, you're so fast."
Me? I'm poky.

Grandma made my sweater.
How do I feel?
Cozy.

Billy laughs at my sweater.
Steve doesn't like it.
How do I feel?
Mad. And sad, too.
My grandma made it for me.

I can write my whole name.
How do I feel?
Smart.

Eddie's not fast at writing.
I tell him, "Good, Eddie. You can do it, too."

I forgot my hat.
I left it at school.
How do I feel?
Stupid.

That Eddie!
Don't you ever forget anything, Eddie?

Grandma needs help.

Wait, Grandma. Let me help.

Grandma gives me a bag.
How do I feel?

STRONG!

I stop the dog.
He's bothering my kitty.
How do I feel?
Brave.

Get away, dog!

The big dog gives a big bark.
How do I feel?
Scared.

Aren't you scared, Eddie?

My brother Mike helps me.
How do I feel?
Safe.
I'm not scared anymore.

Guess what—
we won the ball game!
How do I feel?
Big. Like Mike.

We all go inside.
How do we feel?
Tired and dirty.

Want to take a bath, Eddie?

Grandpa and Grandma have a fight.
How do I feel?
Worried.

Eddie's worried, too.

Look at Grandma and Grandpa!
Now they're friends again.

How do I feel?
Better.
Everybody feels better.

Tomorrow's our birthday, Eddie.
How do you feel?

Special, very special.

Me, too.

How do we feel?

Happy!

Norma Simon grew up in Brooklyn, the Bronx, and Manhattan, but she and her husband, Edward Simon, and their children prefer a Cape Cod home where life can still seem somewhat removed from city tensions.

When she was a little girl, Norma Simon liked roller skating and jumping rope, but reading and writing were her favorite activities. Pretending was fun, and in writing one could pretend all sorts of things. Her first published book appeared in 1954 and was followed by many others, often for young children, but including one semi-autobiographical story for girls.

Norma Simon earned her first degree from Brooklyn College and an M.S. in Education from the Bank Street College of Education in New York City. She is on the Bank Street staff as an educational consultant. Experience in preschool teaching and in planning Headstart programs has made Mrs. Simon especially aware of books that deal meaningfully with everyday life. Her **What Do I Say?** and **What Do I Do?** were written with this need in mind and are available in both English and English with Spanish.

Joe Lasker won his first art prize, a medal, when he was a third grader in Brooklyn. Even then he knew that he wanted to be an artist and nothing else. He attended the Cooper Union Art School in New York City but his career was delayed by service in World War II. When he resumed painting, he won Prix de Rome and Guggenheim fellowships that made possible study in Europe and Mexico. His paintings are in museum collections, and he has had numerous one-man shows in New York and Philadelphia.

Some of the characteristics of Joe Lasker's easel paintings are evident in his illustrations for picture books. He brings a welcome masculinity and a humorous way of seeing things that children enjoy. His studio is in his home in South Norwalk, Connecticut. His wife, Mildred, teaches perceptually handicapped children. David, Laura, and Evan are the Laskers' three children.